Tá Cathal Ó Searcaigh in ard a chumais, é éirithe ó thalamh as an duibheagán. Is aoibhinn liom na bundánta, an charthain iontu a mheall riamh sinn chun nádúir na Gaeltachta.

Liam Ó Muirthile

In Cathal Ó Searcaigh's poetry, the unexpected rises to the surface like foam formed under a waterfall during the spring thaw. His poetry is both startling and refreshing, celebrating love, friendship, and the draw of poetic kinship in lines like the following that invoke Walt Whitman: "You beheld the spirit's playful spume in oceans, the spill/ of a boy's seed on starstruck autumn nights." Or "Protect me from evil detractors, the pigeon-hearted and the/ righteous, the scary whited sepulchures." His images are crisp and concrete: "Her hair was a copper cascade/ in free fall; a river of light/ in full spate". But behind their polished surfaces lurks the mythic depth of Blake in poems like 'The Language Tree'. These translations sparkle.

Bill Wolak

Cavafy knew well that his poems would not be acceptable to his contemporaries; but he was prepared to pay the price and carried on. How gratifying, then, for admirers of the homoerotic tradition in poetry and in art generally, to see that the tide is finally turning —and for those of us who take an interest in Irish, to see also the international setting that the language has found for itself in Cathal Ó Searcaigh's most recent work.

Eoghan Mac Aogáin

Out of the Wilderness

Cathal Ó Searcaigh

Ⓟ The Onslaught Press

Published in Oxford by The Onslaught Press
11 Ridley Road, OX4 2QJ
September, 2016

☮

The poems in this edition were orininally published in Irish by
Cló Iar-Chonnachta (in *Gúrú i gClúidíní* 2006 & *An Bhé Ghlas* 2015) and
Arlen House (in *An tAm Marfach ina Mairimid* 2010, *Aimsir Ársa* 2014 & *Na Saighneáin* 2014)
and are © **Cathal Ó Searcaigh**

ISBN: 978-0-9956225-2-4

Typeset in Akira Kobayashi's **Din Next** & Christ Burke's **FF Celeste**,
designed & edited by **Mathew Staunton**

Printed and bound by Lightning Source

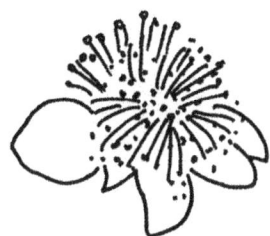

Introduction

The Poems

from *Gúrú i gClúidíní, 2006*

from *An tAm Marfach ina Mairimid, 2010*

from *Aimsir Ársa*, 2014

from *Na Saighneáin*, 2014

from *An Bhé Ghlas*, 2015

Essay

Introduction

Voice in the Wilderness/ Guth san Uaigneas

Art was at the beginning of time, prayer.
Wood and rock were truth.

Tristan Tzara (Sic, Sep. - Oct., 1917)

What makes great poetry? An unmistakable voice, what else, one that is attuned to the creative intelligence of the universe, responding to the eternal questions with all that is distilled from a life lived by a sensitive enquiring mind, a mind that has absorbed the best of what the native tradition can offer, a mind open to world literature, a mind inhabiting an organism that lives and breathes in a particular environment, now, but subtly aware of the human condition before this brief encounter with time. A poet of now, yesterday and of ages to come, aware of his destiny as a poet.

We recognise the work of a mature Cezanne, van Gogh, Klee or Chagall, do we not? We look at a painting and say to ourselves, 'It could be no other!' It is the same with Ó Searcaigh. There is none other like him. An intimate voice in the wilderness. A phrase, a word, a pause, and we know it can be none other than he. I find this recognition factor to be a reliable touchstone when separating wheat from chaff. (Pardon the mixed metaphor). Much of what I read in poetry journals is unrecognisable or, as Mumbai poet Hemant Divate has remarked, cloning! Much of today's poetry offers little by way of spiritual sustenance and, so, will be forgotten. In his *Literary Essays*, Thomas Merton says of the true poet that

> he seeks above all to put words together in such a way
> that they exercise a mysterious and vital reactivity among
> themselves, and so release their secret content of
> associations to produce in the reader an experience that
> enriches the depths of his spirit in a manner quite unique ...

Reading Ó Searcaigh, we know we are reading poetry. This may sound obvious but the distinction between poetry and prose has become blurred. Aurobindo says:

> ... the first aim of prose style is to define and fix an object, fact, feeling, thought before the appreciating intelligence with whatever clearness, power, richness or other beauty of presentation may be added to that essential aim; the first aim of poetic style is to make the thing presented living to the imaginative vision, the responsive inner emotion, the spiritual sense, the soul-feeling and soul-sight.

Ó Searcaigh's voice is the true voice of poetry, one that makes the matter of his poems 'living to the imaginative vision'; living, yes; a voice in the wilderness, it cannot live anywhere else. *Slí an uaignis* is the path to poetry, as Aogán Ó Rathaile testifies.

> a glimmer
> from a rusty nail in the door—
> November sun

Ó Searcaigh's prophecy is beauty, the broad canvas as much as the haiku vision above. Like Keats, he knows the truth of beauty, from experience, and knows that beauty is forever. I quote now from an unlikely source:

> Poets are like the landscape; there even though no one is looking. Without them, man would not exist. Poets appear when drizzle or nostalgia, joyful spring, truth or deep sorrow, prick the conscience. Then they search the layers of your soul like an electrician after a storm, tying cables, changing fuses, isolating bare wires with a cloak of verse. Like a covering of snow over the landscape, smoothing out the bumps, levelling the hidden depths, opening the distances to memory. And making the sun sparkle in their reflections. There have always been poets, their metaphors making magic of facts, with that

existential wisdom they seem to be born with. What is more, poets are always poor and, even if they may one day get published successfully, they retain that touch of tenderness that men who make fortunes do not possess...

Che Wants to See You, Ciro Bustos (Verso, 2013)

Cathal has never been much of a political animal and wouldn't have time for Che Guevara, or guerrilla fighters at home or anywhere in the world, but he would be interested to know and be consoled by the fact that a wilderness voice is heard in the unlikeliest of places. Cathal's voice is being heard now, at home and across the world, and will always be heard wherever poetry is loved and needed.

Trudging through the crackling, bone-crunching Bolivian jungle, Bustos heard some strange noises:

> On a flatter stretch, where walking was easier, the mystery revealed itself. The noise began taking shape: I could hear words, harmonious, suggestive, beautiful rhythmic words. It was Che reciting poems by León Felipe as he walked.

Poetry has sustained Cathal Ó Searcaigh in the jungle, in the wilderness of life—and sustained his readers, sustained them with the sheer beauty and naturalness of his language, his vision, compassion and hope, the intoxicating power of his love (sacred and profane), his illumination of a singing landscape, only matched in modern times by Sorley MacLean, that other prince of Gaeldom, both of them orphic voices in the wilderness.

It's not altogether true that he is an apolitical poet, of course, and his 'A Postcard to Yusuf in Iraq' (p.42) deserves a place in any anthology of anti-war poems. See also the two poems here from *An Bhé Ghlas* (pp.115 & 116) Furthermore, writing in a lesser-spoken language is a political act, of sorts, in itself. It asserts the beauty, the integrity and the dignity of those lives which find voice and meaning far from the madding crowd.

He is politically vocal, as well, without naming and shaming anybody, when he describes the desolation of many Gaeltacht areas due to unemployment and emigration and our seeming inability as a people and as a nation to maintain (not to mention revive) the Irish language.

If disappointment and anger can be sensed in many poems, there is, too, an acceptance, an acceptance which is greater than his defiance, as in the delicately phrased poem 'Mountain Trek' (p.54), which seems to suggest that everything is all for the good. A poet has no choice but to accept his vocation and to sacrifice his life to it, his joy, his sorrow, his journeys into the unknown. In *Na Saighneáin* (2014) we find an acceptance tinged with melancholy—and, not for the first time, a philosophical look at the world, in its bloom and decay, that somehow reminds me of the great poetry of the T'ang Dynasty, a poetry often tinged with longing, regret and exile in which only the grandeur of nature can offer some little measure of solace. One of these poets, Wang Wei, says:

> In late years I desire only peace,
> for worldly affairs my heart has no concerns . . .

In Cathal's meditations, in which language and landscape interweave, mystically, music never deserts him. The music in the poetry of Ó Searcaigh and MacLean is ancestral, vital, essential. This euphony contributes in no small way to their greatness and defines the colour and timbre of their distinctive utterances. Their use of language could be said to be 'broaching the ineffable' as L. Kramer says in *Music and Poetry: The Nineteenth Century and After* (1984).

Euphony is literally 'good sound'. It has been there since the cradle of civilisation, whether intoned or internalised. Its loss in the modern world, particularly in the Anglosphere, is the main cause, I would suggest, of poetry's increasing marginalisation and irrelevance. (A similar loss occurred with the exit of Latin from the Roman Catholic liturgy. The new liturgy in English does not have the poetic, sonorous wherewithal to soar, as Latin soars, as Irish soars).

Let's listen! The following lines from a quatrain have the simplicity, innocence and musicality of Tagore (in the aphoristic pieces found in the Bengali's *Stray Birds*, for instance):

> Éiríonn na focla as mo chroí
> ina n-éanacha uaigneacha trá
>
> *Words fly up from my heart*
> *lonely birds from the beach*

The second line in Irish with its é/ú/á sounds is typical of the magnetic appeal of Gaelic versecraft and often comes natural to Irish-language poets who are steeped in the genius of the ancient tradition. The Anglo-Saxon tradition does not have the same vowel play and tends towards closing off a phrase or a word with consosants. The lines above, as found also in Romance languages, are lines in which vowels matter and remain open.

Expanding further on this note, look at the word 'Mozartian' as used by Máire Mhac an tSaoi in *The Southern Review* to describe Ó Searcaigh's poetry:

17

Ó Searcaigh is Mozartian, following the Gaelic classical convention of the dramatic first person, which disinfects the 'I', moving easily from traditional metres to free verse and back, distilling the intense emotions of same-sex love into a lyric form that has not, I think, been equalled since the days of the Greek Anthology.

'Mozartian' also suggests, to me, an intricate sonic web that sounds familiar, easy, effortless to our ear, in spite of its invisible complexity; 'Mozartian' suggests, too, a surge and fall of sound exactly as it should be, and an experience that will repay frequent listening. So it is with the ethereal and healing music of Ó Searcaigh's poetry.

The translator's task in the case of Cathal Ó Searcaigh revolves around absorption and recreating or transcreating what is experiencable in the original. By absorption we mean, in this instance, entering the life of the poem, hypnotically, through the river of sound. In this regard, all translations of Irish poetry fall short of the mark and are nothing but sign language for the deaf. As there are so few readers of Irish-language poetry today, who—we may well ask—is the poet addressing? Ghosts, much of the time, fellow poets, artists and scribes from other ages, other climes, or young victims of violence in the Middle East; or he addresses entities which cannot understand his language, such as Mount Errigal. Only the crass materialist, the rationalist, would say that the above are indifferent to his utterances.

The English translator of Ó Searcaigh can never forget that he is fashioning something in what is, after all, the historically imperialist language, a language which threatens to swallow the Irish language and his own sub-dialect. Indeed, he may well be the very last speaker of the Irish of Mín 'a Leá. Fortunately, we have recordings of his beautiful voice.

****

Enlightenment, says Dogen, is intimacy with all things. Such intimacy is an impossibility for many, impossible even to imagine, cut off as we are from Nature and from ourselves.

Fuinneog

I mo shuí anseo go beo
ag amharc amach ar chaoráin fraoigh, ar phortaigh,
tig lí chorcra ar mo bhriathra, ar mo smaointe;
bogann mo chroí leo

Window

I sit here and I am alive
looking out at tufted heather on the moor
words and thoughts are purple-hued
in and among them the heart thrives.

But, of course, as we see in the poem 'Enclosed Fields' (p.35), nothing is permanent, all is flux:

Over beyond the cliff
I can see enclosed fields
head over heels . . .

When we listen to Cathal, recorded or live, in the best of his fully realized poems we can hear our mother, our mother tongue, our lover, a mountain stream, a breeze in the barley field, some pure and natural sound, some euphony, some 'good sound' as though for the first time; we are giving ear to an ancestor we have never known, listening to a pure sound that comforts us now, that steals our heart and gives it back again, a heart that is more alive now than ever before because it has known the depths of another heart.

19

He wasn't long out of short trousers when I first met him and I freely announced to whoever might have been listening that a major poet was in the making and would soon be leaving his mark. We didn't have long to wait. Cathal has fulfilled his promise a thousand times over. True poet that he is, he can tackle any mood, any form, the lyric, the long poem 'Mount Errigal' (p.83), odes to Whitman (p.56), Isherwood (p.104) and Mandelstam (p.109), the haiku.

In my book *Haiku Enlightenment*, I singled out the following haiku as a perfect example of sabi:

> speal mo sheanathar
> ag meirgiú sa scioból—
> clapsholas fómhair
>
> *my grandfather's scythe*
> *rusting in the barn—*
> *autumn twilight*

By *sabi* (from the verb 'sabir' to rust) we usually mean that aura or patina of loneliness surrounding some old or revered object, or a hallowed place steeped in antiquity. Daisetz Suzuki, however, sees *sabi* as linking us to the world of childhood and to a purer experience of reality than grown-ups can ever know. I would suggest that this is what Cathal Ó Searcaigh and his poetry is all about—and it is true, as well, of many other great poets whose work I admire. He is perfectly placed in the hills of Donegal, those hills that called him back home from London, from the pub where he worked, the Ox and Gate between Cricklewood and Neasden, to contemplate reality in all its endless guises. The pub still exists. We should take it over some time for an evening of reminiscing, poetry and wassail!

A keen sense of *sabi* links him to the world of childhood, the world in which he first tasted the strands of tradition, traditions that until very recently formed and shaped rural Gaelic society; the childhood of his father's seasonal migrations to Scotland, the childhood and youth of his unhappy experiences at National School, his same-sex awakenings of physical desire. It may be that a psycho-sexual union unfulfilled in adolescence remains forever unfulfilled and can only be sublimated at a later stage by some form of mystical or pantheistical union. See 'Sunshimmers' here, (p.59).

Ó Searcaigh's sexual-spiritual energy is Whitmanesque—no dualistic divisions here between spirit and body. He is also Wordsworthian:

> Embrace me then, ye Hills, and close me in.
> Now in the clear and open day I feel
> Your guardianship . . .
>
> ('The Recluse')

We are not a thousand miles away from Mín 'a Leá.

The world of childhood is also the childhood of his relationship with Agnes, his fairy-ridden mother, the mother movingly described in his memoirs *Light on Distant Hills* in a chapter which I discuss in an essay appendixed to this volume, the mother whose presence (and *absentia* in fairydom) he misses greatly in the touching, brilliant elegy 'Hair Pins' (p.60); a childhood of landscape and place lore which are characteristic of Gaelic poetry in Ireland and Scotland throughout the ages, a landscape celebrated with the fervour of the first poets whose task it was to name the physical environment in detail so that we would know where we find ourselves and the lore associated with our little patch of earth. Whitman, so often evoked by Ó Searcaigh, preferred the native name, Panmonok, to Long Island. The placenames in Heaney's poetry, Glanmore, Moyola, Anahorish, Mossbawn are well loved, certainly, but distorted by the prism of Anglicisation; they are all one step removed from their original fire and, for this reader at any rate, are lacking in primal incandescence, in the authentic meaning, shape, sound, story and truth found in Mín 'a Leá, Gort na mBan Sí, Abhainn Mhín an Mhadaidh, Dúnán, Gort an Choirce, Cnoc an tSéideáin, Caiseal na gCorr, Log Dhroim na Gréine, Mín an Lábáin, Carn an Traona and dozens more. These names come off our lips with the same delight as we might experience them in the great *Fiannaíocht* poetry or even in *The Táin* itself.

The celebration of placenames (in their authoritative form) is also part of the sabi of Ó Searcaigh (as it is of Sorley MacLean), a link not only to childhood but to antiquity and when we hear these names, as Irish speakers, we hear a meaning and a music as old as the hills. As the anonymous minstrel said:

> Cnoc an Áir an cnoc seo thiar
> Is go Lá an Bhrátha beidh á ghairm;
> A Phádraig na mbachall bán
> Ní gan fáth a tugadh an t-ainm...
>
> (*Hill of Slaughter the hill to the west*
> *Until the crack of doom so will be its name;*
> *Patrick of the white croziers*
> *Not for nothing it earned its fame*)

It must be said that with Ó Searcaigh and Heaney, different sensibilities are at work. There's a poem by Ó Searcaigh (in fact there are several in this mode) called 'A dhúiche m'anama'/ 'Region of my spirit', a poem too luscious to translate in which from a distant clime the poet makes love to the native landscape. I am reminded of the sensory landscape of Indian aesthetics in which the environment is seen and felt as a refracted Krishna. Yeats knew what he was talking about when he said that before the Battle of the Boyne, Ireland belonged to Asia. Did not Irish kings engage in

22

public intercourse with a white mare, the horse symbolising the land itself, as in India a queen pantomimed sex with a dead stallion? (Let's not tell the tabloids about this).

My repeated reference here to antiquity, some will say, is twaddle. But people often miss the obvious, such as the very title of Cathal's 2013 volume *Aimsir Ársa* which means 'Antique Times', nor can we forget the sequence surrounding the bold Tuathal in the 2010 volume, *An tAm Marfach ina Mairimid*, a sequence which is the most convincing and scintillating recreation, or pastiche, of medieval verse-craft imaginable.

Like the Greek-American poet, Nicolas Calas, he embraces the past with non-nationalistic fervour and, of course, his dreams and visions are pre-national and will be celebrated in post-national times to come. Calas says:

> I envied the cold stones
> Standing here still for ages
> Listening to the sweet echoes of past excitement . . .

How much closer Cathal is, intellectually and tempramentally, to the Greeks—to Calas and Cavafy, let us say—than he is to Ó Direáin and Ó Ríordáin. And Calas (who had worked with anthropologist Margaret Mead) would be more than a little interested in poems such as 'Crann na Teanga'/ 'The Language Tree' (p.46) which is Druidic, shamanic, and genuinely so. In this poem, and in many others, Ó Searcaigh asserts the sacredness of language and, in so doing, reminds us of the unconscionable sacrilege which is linguicide. *Sabi* —that useful word again!—can, I believe, link us to the primordial, to the mytho-poetical realms of prehistorical lore and legend. See, for instance, the prose poem 'Nocturnal Vision in a Foreign Land' (p.41). It's not one of his best-known poems, perhaps because it's a prose

23

poem. There are few prose poems in the modern Gaelic canon. (We have the splendid 'Meáchan Rudaí' by Liam Ó Muirthile; but who can think of many more)? 'Nocturnal Vision in a Foreign Land' contains the word *fís* or 'vision'. We often associate 'vision' and 'visionary' with looking into the future. But a true visionary can also look into the past. We need visionaries in both directions, now and always.

Of course, 2014 saw the publication of another new volume from Cathal in which the prose poem is given pride of place. That book is *Na Saighneáin* which can mean 'the Northern Lights' or celestial phenomena of every description and the book commences with an act of sun worship. When we dance a reel, are we not re-enacting those circular dances of our ancestors in praise of the Sun, something which the Dervish does, too, in his own way?

> Ní i nDia atá mo dhóchas
> ach sa tsolas . . .
>
> *My hope is not in God*
> *but in the light . . .*

Let's be clear about this: Cathal's poetic territory is pre-Christian and when Philp O'Leary refers to him (in *The Irish Literary Supplement*) as 'the contemporary voice of an unbroken tradition', we must understand this to encompass pagan beginnings, long before Patrick attempted a replacement of the Sun with the Son.

What Standish O'Grady once said of Whitman can be said of Ó Searcaigh:

> For you to-day who read my poems he reminds us, this noble planet
> that travels round the sun gradually cohered from the nebulous
> float, and passed through all its initial and preparatory stages. He

must be of importance for whose reception preparations so vast, 'preparations that extended through millions of years', have been undergone. Now at last the guest has arrived, and that guest of the Universe is the reader . . .

Cathal's introduction to my own new and selected poems was dated 'Oíche Shamhna', the Celtic opening into the Otherworld. Do not imagine that such a date was arbitrary. It validates my thesis, namely that the Gaelic tradition is incredibly alive and open to realms which are off the radar of the dominant culture, the Anglosphere. (No need to labour the point. It's the poetry that matters in the end).

The poems translated here were all published after Cathal's own dogged jungle trek, suffering as he did the modern-day equivalent of the rack—trial by media. That period spent in the furthest reaches of the wilderness, so tangibly expressed in 'Ovid Speaks' (p.72), was one of internal exile. Whether as an act of self-defence or one of defiance, poetry can be a powerful talisman and we can only marvel at the resilience of the man and the poet who emerged from that jungle chastened, yes, but singing as never before, drawing immense spiritual, cultural and poetic strength from his native heath among the hills of Donegal and from the living dead, from deserted townlands, a physical and psychic environment in all its unique majesty and frailty.

What keeps him going? What keeps his poetry going? What keeps the Irish language going? What else but access to the shadowy world. Call it the fairy world and the term will be misconstrued as a neo-Celtic Twilight. The shadow-world is what it is and what it always was; it does not obey clock or market, or the rules of time and space; it is a world beyond the reach of the media in which the Gaelic psyche explores its myriad uncertainties as the rest of the world digs deeper into its own crumbling certainties.

25

The fairy faith is older than time and so can do with time as it likes. Its home is the wilderness, outside Cathal's door. As W. Y. Evans-Wentz says in *The Fairy-Faith in Celtic Countries*:

> ... the natural aspects of Celtic countries, much more than those of most non-Celtic countries, impress man and awaken in him some unfamiliar part of himself ... which gives him an unusual power to know and to feel invisible, or psychical, influences ...

As with Shinto, this subtle relationship with the environment is what gives life, terror and beauty to the wind, the grass, the rivers, the lakes and rocks. In this sense, our poet of the wilderness is timeless, ancient, ever-new, a creature of our own era and of the Iron Age:

> Ag gríosú smaointe chun spréiche
> Ag casúracht go hard
> Caint mhiotalach mo dhaoine
>
> *Stirring thoughts to flame*
> *Hammering loudly*
> *The mettlesome speech of my people*
>
> [Trans. Gabriel Fitzmaurice]

Ó Searcaigh does not need to return to the Source—he is in and of the Source. This is what Eliot had to say in *The Athenaeum* (Oct. 17, 1919):

> The maxim, Return to the sources, is a good one. More intelligibly put, it is that the poet should know everything that has been accomplished in poetry (accomplished, not merely produced) since its beginnings—in order to know what he is doing himself.

In Ó Searcaigh's work, we have radical new beginnings. ('Radical' means nothing more than a return to roots, from Latin *radix*). And that, too, is the mark of a great poet, one who reinvents himself and renews the language, at Source.

The Poems

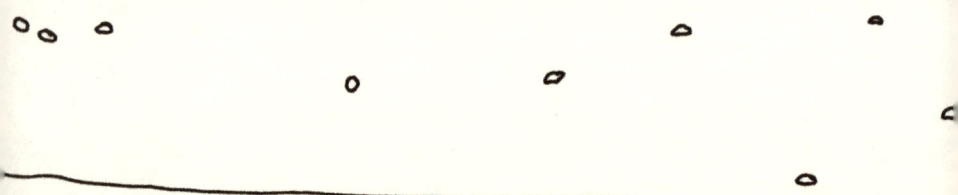

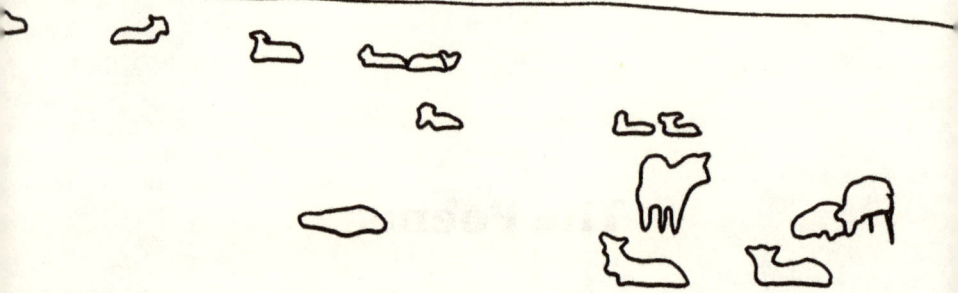

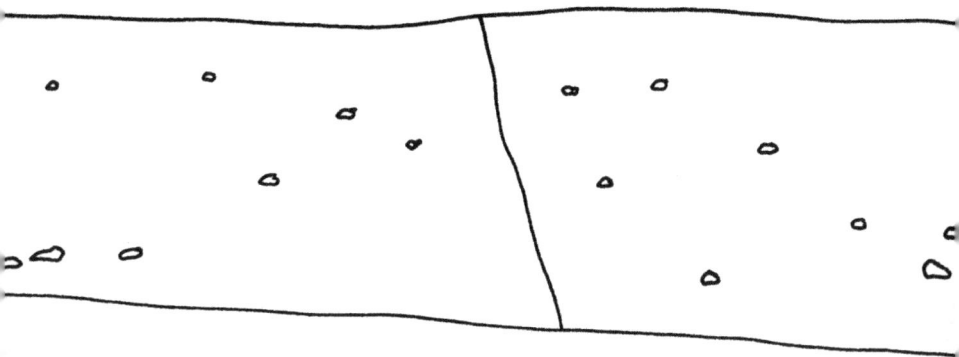

from *Gúrú i gClúidíní*, 2006

Enclosed Fields

Over beyond the cliff
I can see enclosed fields
head over heels.
Were it not for the sheep
ensconced there, pressing down
like paper weights,
they would be as leaves
swept away
into nothingness

Kathmandu and her affairs

Day breaks out and she wakes me up suddenly
With a cock-crow kiss!
Looking out from the top window
I spy her in the streets, parading her morning saffron sari.
Her breath in traffic flow, pure draught of heat.

She's on her feet now, no time to rest,
Her clutch about her;
She rouses them with a noisy jackdaw voice, puts the skids under them,
Humouring them so that they might face this day breezily—
A day rising out from the yellowing globe of her eye.

Lunch hour, from the hotel balcony, I see her
Stretched in slumber,
Her urban contours lying awkwardly, dog tired,
Her bazaar bosom heaving, exhausted,
The dangerous laneways of her combed tresses.

Today the poor are huddled
In the backstreets of her cloak, fretful,
Their wants, their needs pierce her
And how she sighs over and over again when the strong
Walk all over the weak—kid goat teaching its mother to bleat.

Tutelary spirit of street shrines, wonder-woman of broken palaces,
Wise one of crumbling courtyards.
A while ago her sky-eyes darkened and she wept with consternation
Seeing her family rising up in rebellion
Against all oppressors.

The softness of prayer in her wild words
As her body supports scaffolding—
Stink of pus in her bones—
In spite of this she sings a song of hope
In the cries of protesters, blossoming tongue of youth.

Evening. Pagoda-shaped she is,
Bright gems glisten in her ears;
She walks a stately walk among her own, blesses them
With incense chatter: hear the little peals of laughter
As she banters with market ladies, fiery eyed.

Night. She spreads the bright
Head-dress of darkness
Over all, her satin cloak
Encrusted with silver brooches, an amber moon
Her torch, traffic horns her hum.

To her I will lift my eyes, my soul's nurse,
When midnight rings
And I stretch my limbs; she comes to me with a sleeping-draught
Full of giddy sparks from the sky. As she departs
She leaves a star in the window, sweet and soft as her kiss.

When my name you spoke

When my name you spoke, my love,
in soft sighs of affection, it was not my name
any longer but the flowering sword lily
yellowing in the mouth of the breeze.
When to your heart you pressed me
wildly, I was no more, I became
a summer stream
welling up and breaking its banks.

Words Fly Up

Words fly up from my heart
lonely birds from the beach
seeking shelter for the night
in love's green branching reach.

Window

Sitting here I am alive
tufted heather on the moor
words and thoughts are purple-hued
among them the heart thrives

Nocturnal Vision in a Foreign Land

I cannot rid my mind of them, white swans a-coming. For aeons numberless, exiled in dark, in grey-blue loneliness swimming. Show them some pity, they say, and they will find their human form again. On my tears a-coming white swans, each neck more beautiful than a lime-washed mansion in moonlight. How can I refuse them, bright plumage falling, in human form a-coming.

A Postcard to Yusuf in Iraq

A balmy March night in Manhattan
I stand at the doorstep
where you once lived in Bleeker Street
and where I loved you in the eighties.
I linger at this door into delight,
the moon-madness of our embraces comes flooding back
and how we spoke of your homeland—
the sunny stretches between Najaf and Hillah.
Where are you tonight? I don't know,
the foundations of the world shiver, beloved,
from Najaf to Hillah; your people tremble
beneath a mighty hail of cowardly assault.
Bombs of the barbarians rain on you
and your cities are ruins, your towns and villages destroyed,
and I fear greatly that your life may be in peril
as they come to lay waste to what lies between Najaf and Hillah.
Tonight as I linger at the door to my heart's desire
thinking of you and of something you once said:
'The poet's homeland is in the hearts
of the oppressed.' Tonight, beloved,
what can I say but assure you
in a language not heard above tumult and confusion
that I am with you, entirely. The bomb
is victorious over my word and the missile mocks my poem,
but tonight I am with you, my treasure of all Iraq
for your heart, throbbing there in the crimson fire of war,
is my homeland, my poem, my humanity.
And so, man of my heart and soul,
I am with you now from the crown of my head
in Najaf to the soles of my feet in Hillah.

December

Summer visitors have gone away
the cuckoo and the corncrake
southwards flown to warmer climes
but you, dear one, have stayed behind,
little robin, chirping
on December's threshold bare.
All alone the two of us here
singing songs lustily
red-breasted songs defying doom—
a sod aflame in the heart
of wintry gloom.

Shadow

I'm at your heels
alive
tied
to your destiny
forever
I'm your shadow
the lighter side
of your self
the side
which flows
from the well of sunshine
in your mind.
I am your shadow
tightrope walker of the moon
pooka of your phantasmagoria
walking the vertical walls
of night
I contain brightness
and darkness
dancing spark of life
and artic cold
of death
here I am
in the middle of the day
on the flat of my back
on Market Street
and yourself upstanding
in the queue for vegetables
multitudes stamping on me
and me without a twitter of wit
unable to scream aloud
and look for mercy.

Other times
it's so full of myself
I am
that I become
gigantic
and frighten you
a spectral shape
by your side
giving you
the heebie jeebies
I am your shadow
the dark side
of your self.
You're going to have to
deal with me
before you enjoy
the bliss of light
in your self.
At the hour of death
our destiny
is to merge
and be whole
and I won't venture out
of you any more
I'll plant myself in you
like a seed
as you grow
in eternity

The language tree

I see the land once more. The rounded territory envisioned.
Pale-green hills standing between life's storms and the face
of eternity. Secret kingdom of youth.
Our tongues had knowledge and were prophetic,
initiated by the mouths of generations speaking through the elements.
A violent tongue that first took shape in the lightning creation
of the universe.
It was there we understood the coarse vocabulary of the badger,
the veiled talk of jackdaws. We conversed with what was hardly there.
Sweet was our prattle with the hills.
And there was always a tree. The airy tree of the Good Folk.
The tree it was that nourished our language, the wise ones declared,
that gave it meaning and lifefulness, that made it sing in dialects.
Syllables—the falling leaves—
and on it, too, evergreen words in a maze of branches.
Always heavy with the lush fruit of metaphor.
Our tree of life, the sap of meaning,
dominated the landscape of our youth. It stood beautifully
between the mountain of light and the smoother land that soothed us.
I see that territory again. It was here I came into this world
in a sunny booley where the muse dwelt between a luminous mountain
and a green tree.
In their shade, words sprouted within me.
Then came misfortune and storm.
The tree withered. The mountain darkened.
Our language was betrayed.
One by one we were all struck dumb.
The clear mountain stream of language that had nourished
everything along its course and quickened every living thing,
the heart went out of it.
My people no longer could put two words together
to communicate with insects and butterflies, animals and angels.
They vanished from our sight and denied our existence.
Our language froze in an ice-age of silence.

We were lost, perished. We lit a fire in the ancestral home,
a little flame of crimson words
that we had stored away in memory.
We gathered round, warming ourselves on twigs of grammar
and tinder of phrases until break of day.
I see that territory again. The listless tree;
death staring out from it; its foliage sunk in
silence; its voice an empty echo.
Since we lost our language we are adrift
in a mountainy wilderness and no ancestral guide to show us
a way out, blind now to our destiny.

ii

My father would sit on the white rock of the *lios*
And contemplate the future of the tribe. Bard of the deserted villages,
sage of sun-speckled hedge school, voice of wisdom.
The world depended on him. It was to him the people came,
those that remained after what had happened, seeking a helping hand.
He was the reader of destiny and storm.
As he sat one day on the rock in contemplation
the Maid of the Mountain came to him and asked him to sing
the lament of the tree.
The brightness of his tears would save us from the ravages of sorrow, she said.
My father lamented the tree in words borrowed from the wail of the wind
through ruins scattered among the hills.
The history of our tribe was heard in that savage keen.
With every leafy syllable that fell from his mouth, a green
glistening could be seen again in the dumb branches of the tree.
He sang the tree to life once more
with the power of his poem that moved sap.
Language blossomed in every branch:
the fresh green sound of hope, and now we await the day
when the silence between us will be broken by shouts of joy.

47

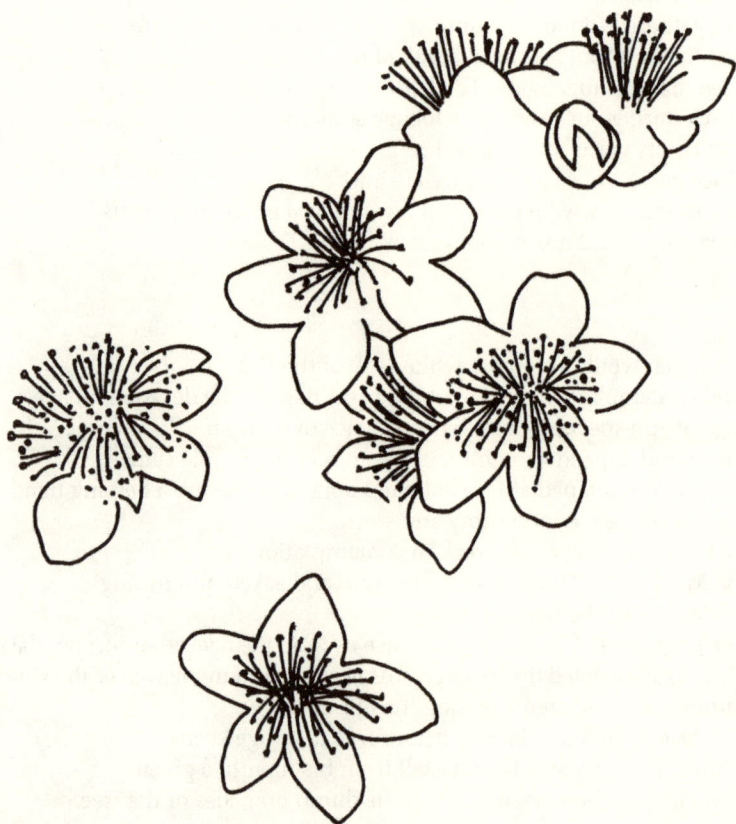

from *An tAm Marfach ina Mairimid,* 2010

Song of Morning

I ask the morning to brighten all that grows
and withers; the snail that pulled through somehow,
The flowers all poisoned. Brighten the ant with its heavy load
Mountaineering among pavement pebbles. Brighten the tree's
Leafy erectness on the building site as it sucks in gunge
From the digger and breathes it out again fresh and clean
In green enthusiasm; brighten the bird that stretches its golden chord
From one tuneful bush to another, roses, cheerful girls
In red skirts perfuming themselves at the lower end of the house;
The golden-eyed daisy that perceives the foot that's going to trample it.

I ask the light to descend on bright things
Struck gloomy, yellow shoe polish, the scent
Of hair, stink of streets, fruits that have grown limp,
The pallid face behind a window, yobbos fighting in the town square,
Milk flowing from the wet-nurse sitting on the lawn, office girls,
The young man in the lounge who described his honeymoon
As honeydoom, no, it wasn't a bed of roses,
Tourists of uncertain hue in the hotel yard, waifs
With bags of glue at the train stop, our daily bread
That I scatter among ducks and deities.

I ask the sun to journey to my heart's desire,
Lie down with him, fondle his core with gold-lacquered fingers,
Kiss his mouth with summery lips, warmly tell him
Of my need for him and though my hopes have gone to seed
I need his love and believe in his gentle ways that ease all pain
So that in spite of everything I can rise up from this immense chasm
And stand on burning slabs, greeting the morning with a poem.

Mountain Trek

Drizzles drench the skin
　furze exudes
　a fragrance

A lull in the conversation
　a bramble
　breaking into flower

A bare mountain pass looms ahead
　a lark above me sweet
　translucent

Living is all there is
　to do now.
　Later

We can find purpose
　pathways
　out of maze & mist

Entering the eye of the storm
　drenching yourself
　in it

In A Grave Time

The sky today translucent
as Buddha's omniscient eye:
a white dove flew by

Its bright angelic wings spelled out
hope—could it be—
hope in this infirmity?

The words were not out of my mouth
when a shot was fired. Sky
an ocean of blood. No lie.

I cannot look up to the heavens
without seeing on the ground
the dove that fell to earth without a sound.

Today, strange as it is to claim,
all the love I have for God
is drowned in that bird's blood.

How can I look any more
at a sky that is gore,
nothing but gore.

To Walt Whitman

for Adil Aouji

As usual, Walt, here I am reading your litany of joy as the grass makes an appearance in Mín 'a Leá.

A shower of rain spurting growth, your words bring the hues and urgency of spring flowing through my imagination.

I can hear your gentle laughter behind the words as I utter your love poems. You need but beckon: what I wouldn't give to be in your arms. I'm not saying we are blood relations, but we are linked by craft and by leanings. Brother, give me your hand, tramp of the road, and we will take words on a walk, with an agile leap of the mind, let's take the air, you take the high road and I'll take the low road and the poem between us.

Brother give me your hand. We'll roam over the vast range of your contemplation and cross the mighty flood of your thought. Out there in the sunny booley of your hope, we'll stretch our limbs awhile in comfort. Let's take the luscious juices from the sun.

Out there in the purple evening of the hills, dear one, we'll discover the America of our desires.

II

Poet of vision, poet of prophecy, green omniscient poet, your camp-fire illumines eternity.

Poetry for you had no boundaries. You were drawn to immensity.

You beheld the spirit's playful spume in oceans, the spill of a boy's seed on starstruck autumn nights.

Beloved god that needed no theology.

Poet of homage. Poet of streaming expansiveness. You honoured the great-hearted order of the cosmos. You could feel the living pulse that nurtured the blade of grass, that conducted the cycle of the spheres. Nothing was too big or too small for your canticle of creation.

You were at home in each limb of the dancing universe.

Your imagination took a seven-league leap from one world to the next. Your poem made safe the path to the abyss.

Your book is as humble as ditch grass, as ambitious as the swell of the sea.

It is my scripture of delight, gospel of joy, full-throated choir, book of wisdom.

III

Your company lifts my heart, Walt, as I run the gauntlet, as blows are struck. The mills of life grind rough and smooth.

Nor was your own life a bed of roses. You had your detractors in their hundreds. And like myself, the love of young men brought you down.

They bad-mouthed you, the evil-hearted ones, proclaiming your poems – your poems exuding grace – were nothing but line after line of vice and temptation.

But you never betrayed your own word. You, the kind-hearted one who couldn't harm a midge, you gave it to them well and good in words of poetry. The wild scream that challenged them in hymns of love. The love that could not speak its name uttered itself in fountains of grace.

Poet all-powerful, caress me now in the sacred bosom of your words.

Protect me from evil detractors, the pigeon-hearted and the righteous, the scary whited sepulchures.

Protect me, Walt, from the gang that tried to take your name away from you. They and their kin are still creating mischief.

Free me from the daughters of treachery and the sons of trickery whose perverted ways have coated my tongue with their scum so that it is hard for me now to raise my voice in the bardic company where I belong.

Give me your gift, Walt, to give every word its true weight, and may every verb strike home so that the barkings of malefactors are rammed back down their throats.

IV

I am reading your litany of delight as grass peeps out in Mín 'a Leá and you, brother, buried in Camden.

But your poem is hale and hearty, voice of spring rising in the green leaves of your humanity.

The world is full of exasperation and malice, and warring factions fill the earth and skies. Factions of faith, tribes of terror!

You saw more than enough of battle gore, Walt, as you nursed soldiers in their final throes, in the bloody years of civil war.

You were reminded, more than ever, as you carried out the corporal works of mercy, that our lot was useless unless we showed what it is to be good neighbours with everyone from Brooklyn to Ballybuddy.

A world of exasperation and malice, Walt, but inspired by your poem I look to the peeping grass; tender grass of brotherhood; rough grass of prophecy; ditch grass of integrity; fragrant grass of truth.

I read your litany of delight, a bad moon on the rise, the bones of the old world have become stale, a new age of misery about to be born. And yet, Walt, lovable brother, you forged a fire that brightens my life tonight. Even now, its glow is palpable.

Your book is the green sod on which I stand alone.

Sunshimmers

Evening and the sun shimmers off the fur of goats . . .
that same shimmer from the soft skin
of boys diving into a river pool.
None can dam the river of time.

Gold-dust gently falls from their skin
glowing with the flame of youth. Young fire!
Nothing is more lonesome than loveliness that fades.
None can dam the river of time.

I see them now swimming, splashing
making noisy fun. In full flower,
already the seeds of decay are sown.
None can dam the river of time.

I listen but the goat bells are too distant now,
lost in hilly dusk. So too,
with surreptitious steps, youth vanishes.
None can dam the river of time.

Hair pins

Your brown knots of hair,
These are hazel brown,
Your tresses bracken and the bracken reddening

Among the remains
of a bowl cast among brambles—
the mouth of the bowl stuffed with earth

Here in the grime behind the house
I discovered hair pins
worn by my mother when I was small

At night her curly brown strands
shone as she tended her hair
combing and brushing

And putting in the pins;
single threads of gold
shining in the light of the tilly lamp

Her hair was a copper cascade
in free fall; a river of light
in full spate

Mammy, your hair stole
the yellow from autumn leaves, softness
from silk, the flash from lightning

The flow from the running stream.
If your ears were my guardian angels
as I lay in the cot,

Your long graceful locks
were God's fingers tickling me
every night before sleep.

If your glistening eyes were soft springs
from which I drank of your healing love,
your flowing head of hair

Was that forest I climbed
to reach the sky, straddling constellations,
my head resting in the bosom of God.

A Winter Night
in a Distant Place

Why, dear one,
do I think of you now
at this juncture of my life?
It must be forty years
if it's a day
since you were my blood brother,
time raced by.

A fine summer's day it was
when first I saw you
on the market street;
your amber hair
primrose hue
firmly astride
your swift steed-motorbike.

Hero of the flashing smile,
sacred tree, brother!
I'd leave my father for you
go far into the distance,
lie with you between hills
on the back of the wind till daybreak.

You noticed me,
noticing you, a youth
of sixteen years at most
bursting with affection for you:
his shining eyes adored you,
ready to elope with you
to netherworlds, mountain pastures.

Such joy was mine
riding from behind

rising in the saddle with you
we braved
the lonely moor
two hands around you
clutching you for all my worth.

Sunny swards amid hummocks
bothies where we kissed, embraced
the lark whistling ever so gaily
I swooned, such was my love
on a fresh bed of leaves
fondling limbs I lived for
you looked me in the eye with pleasure.

Why do I think
of you now
at this juncture of my life?
Forty years
if it's a day
since you were my blood brother
my love, my desire.

There's something lonesome
about standing by yourself
in a back-street laundromat
far away, a winter's evening
listening to the choked growl
of washing machines
turning, turning around.

Much like the years
that slipped us by, sweetheart,
your motorbike brightening the bog road home.

Public Park in Tampere

for Janak Sapkota

I sit on a bench in the town park
on a sunny autumn evening, watching
cyclists and joggers
on their rounds, soaking up the sun
deliciously, limb-stretching with such delight.
       This was once a burial place.
Young mothers stroll along the paths
their offspring sporting among tombs.
Beneath the trees, couples are reaping the harvest of love,
finding themselves in each others arms.
How I love this place. Such joy it brings to the heart
    to see a graveyard like this, dancing with life.

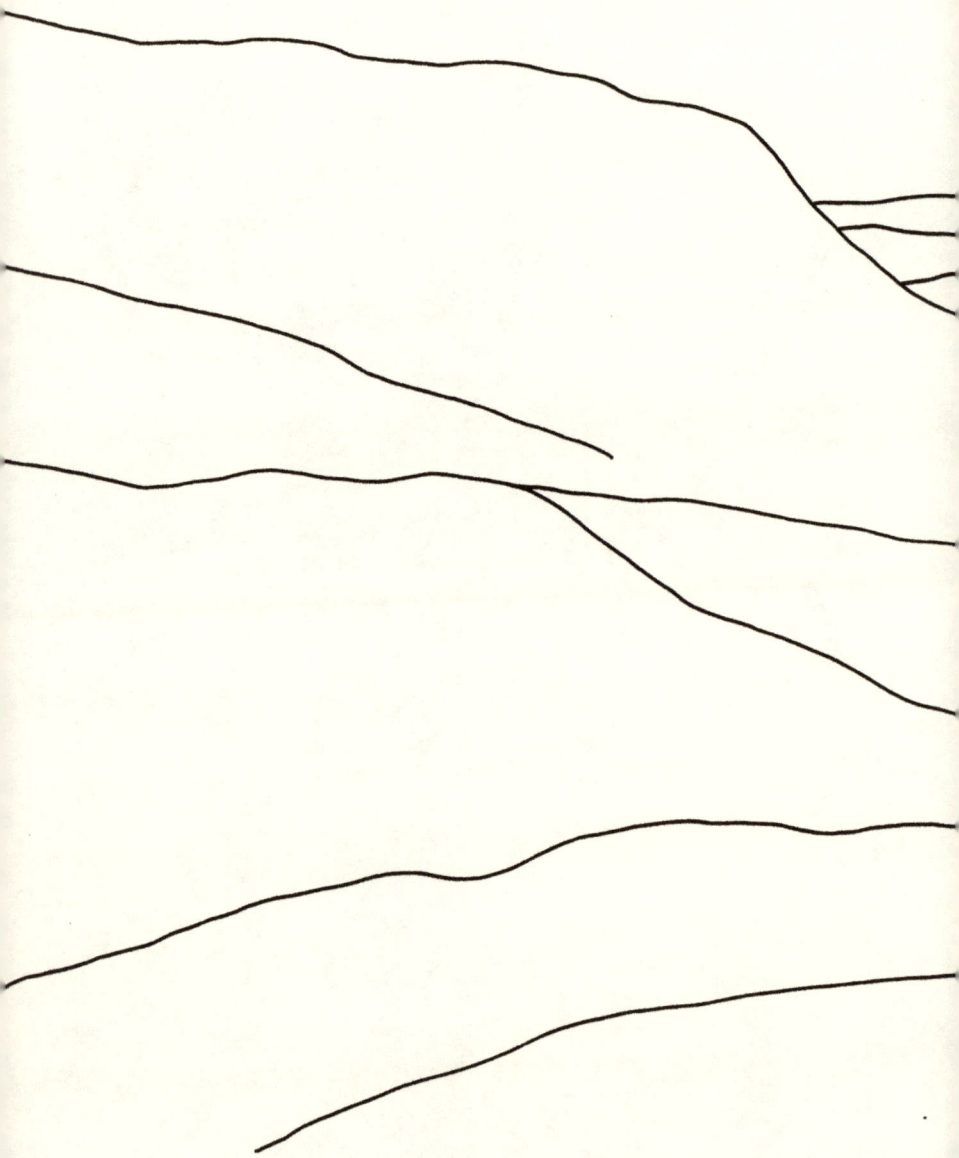

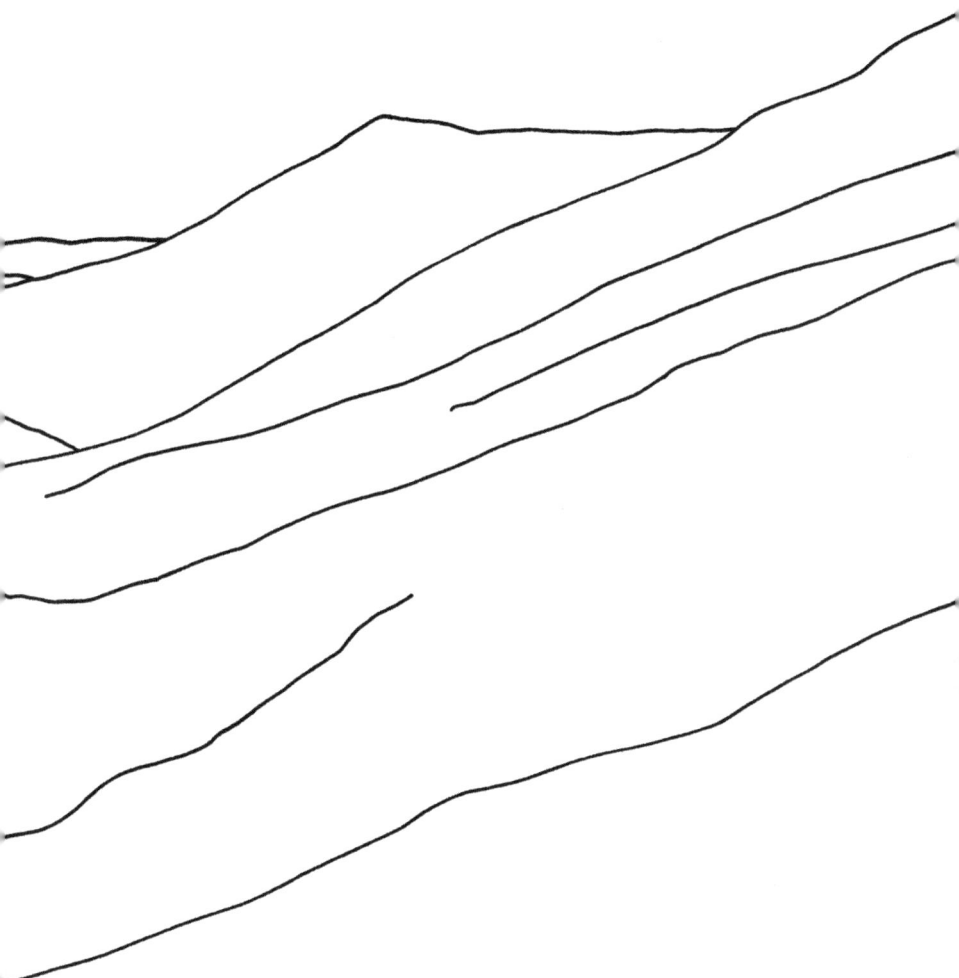

from *Aimsir Ársa,* 2014

Benfeita, Portugal

Here the brightness of sunlight commands me
streaming down from the blue hillocks of sky—
grace and shapeliness of angels from an age gone by.

It sits awhile on humpy red roofs
until it catches its breath once more
after its long journey to earth's shore.

It quietly dips in the river, its regal body—
glistening all over—sings,
and the waters are beatified by its limbs.

It befriends the old lime-washed houses,
nestling among them with an embrace—
see now the vigour where once was a sickly face.

All of its bountiful gifts it spreads evenly, generously,
among olives, grapes and plums; all the while
back gardens are wreathed in a heavenly smile.

When night falls it curls up in the green lap
of trees, slumbers peacefully alone
nodding off to a gentle insect drone.

My love for ever, my fairy wooer
capturing my heart in gold and green
how I trust each glowing atom and stately mien.

And oh how I shall miss you when I go—
for with honey I have been kissed—
bound once more for the foggy isle of mist!

Ovid Speaks

For Frankie Watson

A hundred curses on this place of banishment,
back door to nowhere by the Black Sea.
The warmest day here would freeze the legs off a heron!

It's a far cry from the cosiness and comforts of Rome.
I'm going to seed here among barbarians
with as much learning and table manners between them as a flea.

Oh for a drop of that divine elixir,
fruit of the vine that gives sparkle to words!
For liquor here there's nothing but ice in the bottom of a jug.

Oh for the sunny slopes of those homeland vines again,
olive groves, wooded hills.
There I could live off consonants and vowels.

Scintillating Rome! Always in my thoughts,
where I juggled with life and death. There I gave colour
to humility, boldness to the sweetest sounds.

My brain will snap before I understand this Black Sea blather,
it strikes the ears betimes as the howl of wolves,
other times the wrenching of ice from itself.

Augustus it was who betrayed me and blackened my name,
but harsh though his judgement, his punishment, might seem
I swear he will not have victory over my words.

No king, no regime, however powerful
will tyrannise my poetry now or in times to come.
From age to age my poems will surge. They will speak

To rising generations in the fullness of time;
freemen who couldn't care less about Caesar and his ilk.
This is our age, let him know it, the age of Ovid, Virgil and Horace.

But Augustus is too self-important to see
that it is by the grace of poets that he lives and breathes,
and so will it always be; it is we who fashion the ageless legislation

Of the free word, the honest word that bows not to tyranny,
the glowing commandments of poetry forever guarded by the Muse.
Forgive this hubris, this pride that has brimmed over,

Stature, name and honour have been taken from me
I'm rootless, a beggar. Thrown to the winds
the Word my only home.

Nothing left but to brandish this quill.

Conversation with Li Bai

I am of that age now,
a ripened age
to allow me converse
with you, dear one,
across the black abyss of time.

I sit here sipping wine
under a broad sky.
Autumn, the night is crystal—
your book before me,
wine has knowledge, you say,

and I find nourishment in the golden
flesh of the apple moon
that rounds itself
there on the peak of Errigal.
Wine creates its own verse,

as you know, dear one,
you who abandoned yourself to music and drink.
The divine gutters of poetry!
In that way you freed your mind
from the fetters of this world.

I bow my head to you,
man of merriment,
vagabond of verse, prophet of what came your way,
breaker of all customs, remaining faithful
to nothing but the execution of a poem.

I would like to imagine
our pulse-beat as one
as we both go out to celebrate
a world of no firm standing.
World of trouble! Dream in a bubble!

You lived through hard times,
red with territorial strife,
warring and pillaging wrecked the Kingdom.
You put your hope in poetry,
as I have done, to pull through.

And you took to the wild paths of the world,
wandering clouds accompanied you,
your exclamations of joy heard by passing geese
the moon listened to your earthy ramblings.

Tonight with wine whistling in my blood
I hear the Yellow River of poetry
flowing between the banks of the page.
There you are, flooded in moonlight.
I greet you, with this poem,

across the abyss.

Sunflower

I praise this flower
that blooms in pain
in the unyielding soil of my garden
joyously
facing the sun;
sun seldom seen
in these dark territories of the north,
sunflower filled with homesickness
for bright lands of the south
and all its brothers and sisters
hearts bursting in the heat.

I praise this flower
autumn's delight
blooming before me,
flower of hope
tingling bright
reaching out
to All.
Brother! Bard of light.

Sketch

The grandmother in bed
sharpens her curses
the veins in her wrist

purple as a thundery sky
over the house. The father making music
and gesticulating. The liquor

I gave him has enlivened
his mind. Not a word from the mother
as she spices the food. Their daughter

on the floor sharpening a pencil
with a meat knife, terror in her eyes.
Omar, big brother, settles his hand firmly on my knee

and tells me in a furtive whisper
every time the sky lights up:
"Insha'Allah Charlie! Insha'Allah!"

Deserted Townlands

for Eoin Mac Lochlainn

Evening between two lights
they loom before me
out of the mist that veils generations.

My grandfather, my people's
people, I see them
toiling beneath the sky,

Men reaping in fields of oats
that have long since vanished,
women milking cows

In the sunny booley of Mín
children play hide-and-go-seek
among stooks and sheaves.

As far as the eye can see
the goodly living dead
have all gathered on the old sod,

In the small deserted townlands
of the foothills, in Mín na bPoll,
in Prochlais, in Mín na gCopóg.

Generation after generation, as many
as fill the eye solemnly stride
out of a visionary Mín, and all in the grave.

They pine for old haunts
these townlands
where, day in day out, they toiled.

As quiet as night descending
their footfall
wending their way home

bound to secrecy forever
having wandered the pastures
of the living and the dead . . .

The Melancholic Woman Speaks of the Fairies

In the terrible mountainy loneliness
between Mín na nGall
and Mín na Craoibhe
over from the pathway to the bog
all the way up Malaidh Dhubh
as far as the waters known as Loch na Cuiscrí
there's a forbidden place where airy gentry reside
in all their finery.

But since they have lost their sway
over territories above ground
they have gone from the sight of men
to live out their eternal days in obscurity
between two shades of light
in hideaways
and nooks among whispering lakelets.

And sometimes a fairy blast
will come along and, skipping over its head,
carry with it tufts of heather
down from that yellowing place that leads to Fána Buí
and the excitable fairy folk make a headlong dash
straight out of their enchanted fort:
God bless me now and save me for ever
and let them not sweep me away.

In this hollow where I live
between Mín na nGall and Mín na Craoibhe
all the townlands are blighted, each one,
enclosed fields break out in a rash
trees cough a choking sound
stone walls creak with lumbago

houses have lost their memory.
Last night as I walked in darkness
searching for some comfort along the way
I lost my bearings
having trodden on the sod of confusion
between Mín na nGall and Mín na Craoibhe.
I immediately put my coat on back to front
and when I got to Loch na Cuiscrí
I refused mouth-watering food
from a radiant young man.

Headlines

Headlines of slaughter, horror.
They plunder us, sunder us.
Let the facts of the world
Keep their distance and be still, beloved,
As your tongue explores me
With abundant pleasure.
My treasure, seize the hour. I bow before you,
Sally rod in the wind.

In time to come and sooner than you know
We both will be nothing but names on a headstone,
Numbers in an office file.
Brightness of my life, in time neither of us will breathe
Or think of the other,
And the slaughter will continue,
Gore, killing
As it was from the beginning.

And like ourselves, other lovers
Will experience delirium
On the tip of their tongue,
Headlines of slaughter, horror
Plundering them, sundering them,
As they gleefully seize the hour
Bow to one another, sally rods in the wind
Until nothing is left of them

Names on headstones
Numbers in office files.

Mount Errigal

I

Rarely
do you speak
rapt in contemplation
guru of my adoration.

Once in a while
a koan might slip
from your mouth
as a gift.

Your word is a rock
of weight,
a mystery
to meditate.

Rarely
do you speak
which is why
heather breaks out

In the space between words

II

On sunny evenings
you exude
pure gold
a cascade of loveliness:
alms bestowed
on the poor

III

Warrior
of the windy gap,
hero
filled with battle sap.

Upstanding, faithful, courageous,
our protection, our heart's desire,
fighter of storms
and winter's ire.

Champion of unwavering mind
the moon-shield you hold
in your right, in your left—spear of gold.

Standing erect
in battle fury, wild,
what need we fear?

you are in the gap of danger
ever alert
mountain bare.

IV
You are in love
with the sea
but loath to admit it;
the rolling rollicking wave
speaks to you from day to day
with beguiling sweetness.

Her grey-green lively eyes
bewitch you
bright curve of limbs
tangy breath.
For aeons you hearken
to her flood of chatter
paroxysms of tears.
You can hardly draw a breath
when those buttocks of hers are bared
out there yon by Tory.
You are in love with the sea
and so forever it will be
but here you are
firmly planted in rock
and you'll never go a-roaming with her
west on the boreen.

V

Unlike the sea
in her softness constantly
easily agitated and fiery
of mind and disposition
endlessly roaming the earth
if not above, below

You are of more solid stuff
weighed down by thought.
Unbending in heart, unbending
in mind, you have never known
coming and going out of the blue.
Tough, staunch, no surrender you.

85

But a day will come,
mark my words
the sea will find your soft spot
raging she will come on land—and bloat
and utterly engulf you—
dominatrix of silvery throat!

VI
The sea is a constant bubble of rumour,
mouth ajar!

You are lofty in eternal silence
contemplating the next star.

VII

If you talk at all you talk to yourself alone
poetry of stone.

VIII

When the sun lingers on you
ancient light that comes to us
from afar,
your dull grey
bearded hoariness begins to glow
you are young once more
a million years ago.

IX

Patient
    sovereign
    resolute

courageous
    fearless
        lordly

no words
come near
        your glory

are you not older
 than our own tongue
        than any tongue
            and will you not outlive them all?

X

They believe in you
    rocks
        along sloping fields

You are the Holy One
    All-Powerful
        Lord of All Time

Their only desire and destiny
            is to be with you as once before
        be whole

XI

Formed in Fire you were
at Earth's beginning.

A cinder from that fire
still glows in you,
embers in boulders
flagstones aflame.

The spark is awaiting
judgement day
and will leap forth
from your loins
a mighty blaze
an inferno.

You were born in the fire
in which you will expire.

XII

It is nothing!
You were here before us
you'll be here when we're gone.

XIII

You never knew
God's arrogance.

You are older than He,
this human deity

created
out of fear and neurosis

fear of death
psychosis.

God's arrogance
you never knew

what is man's one-act play
to you?

XIV

Procreative fusion
formed you,
ice carved you,
wind sun
sculpted you
snow rain
polished you
heather gave you features
moss clothed you
bog-myrtle perfumed you
bog-cotton bearded you
lilting you took from the lark
nature gave you permanence
the naturalist, short-lived creature,
pays you homage.

89

XV

Today
I went askew
in the Mám
between yourself
and Cnoc Glas.
Out of my dimensions
outside of time.
It appeared to me
that a garden of chrysanthemums
was blooming
in your shade,
and woods of
cherry trees
were branching out from your peaks,
the air of Japan
had wreathed you in smiles
and Mín na Craoibhe
was in the middle of Kyoto
a woman in a kimono
bowing to you politely.
Was I momentarily duped?
It matters not.
The sage Hokusai was visible to me
on his knees in adoration—
Fuji-Errigal!

XVI

Your gaze constantly
on the world's cycle,
our lives do not horrify you
our deaths do not delight you.

You are not as we are—
fearful toads!—
measuring our life in days
you measure life in stones.

XVII

An autumn evening
from some giddy height
west of Ard na Seamair
I see you wrapping
a lavender cloak
of the loveliest
heathery silk of mountain
around yourself, Oscar.

XVIII
How delicious it would be
to live my life carelessly
in heathery hermitage
windy slopes
sun-embraced peaks
climb you each day
with tender steps.

You are the stairway to sky,
ladder to sun.
I could find the Self
in your crowning light,
understanding would dawn
not from the pages of hoary sages
but from the wind that rushes
over snow

at night in withering March
and from the soft juice of bilberries
in the purple of autumn.
I would chant to elements
and the young morning
adorning you
lauding you
before my open eyes.

How delightful to escape
from the fetters of the world,
free of its wrestling
grip, yell in defiance
on moonstruck
slippery heights.

Like Han Shan
bold pilgrim
aloft
on Cold Mountain,
poet of fiery eye
feral in long endurance
free everlasting
among drifting cloud

XIX

On a a summer evening
as I tread your paths
you are there before me
in peaty pools,
diminutive, sportive,
I could almost
catch you in an embrace
compadre, full of grace.

XX

Have you any memory
of generations who in reverence
spent their lives
labouring and propagating
in good times and bad
here in your shade?

Or have they disappeared
the men and women
who looked up to you
in homage throughout the year
have they gone forever
from the annals of memory?

Are we anything to you?

XXI

A cup of tea
birdsong
a poem or two
if the Muse grants it
alive and well
albeit frugally
and Death—
(who else!)
my only tenant.

And I can't take
my eyes off you
day after day
you draw my gaze
and I contemplate
the way you rise
bravely
from the poverty
of bare-boned earth.

XXII

We ceaselessly seek
to create you
in our own image

Extend you
with metaphor
clarify you

with simile,
fortify you
with symbol.

Why can't we
leave you there
as you are

mountain bare.

XXIII

You are without offspring
as I am too, beloved,
except for the work
all around you, collections
of stones, poems adamantine
born in pain.

Quartz
glitters freely
in poems of praise;
mighty granite
gives weight to laments;
limestone
sharpens satire.

I envy them.
They will live on
when my poems
are mist.

XXIV

Steadying me
when I was rudderless
you resemble Father

Showing kindness
as I rush off into a new life
you resemble Mother

In biting weather
your face obdurate
resembling me

XXV

Each and every inch of you I walked
each brow, each high point, hollow and slope,
rain-washed peak, sun-licked ridge.
I studied everything that grew on you gloriously
your wild flowers & all your healing herbs.

In the pale cloak of March I saw you
in heathery tweed of autumn.
Sun-cloaked in May
in the silky white of January
but the more I gaze the less,

dear heart, I can tell:
such is the fate of those who lie under your spell.

from *Na Saighneáin,* 2014

Harvesting

There you are swinging the scythe
me beside you making the bundles firm,
the two of us harvesting
a sunny evening in Páirc na Díobhóige

The rose-oil of light makes the hills
and the fields all splendid;
you perspire, your beautiful young face
as perfect as an ear of corn, my darling

Soon night will spread its secret cloak
over the narrow gossiping villages
when you and I go harvesting
in our own sweet field together

To Christopher Isherwood

Here I am at your doorstep, a gay pilgrim, Christopher,
this home from home where you sketched the fleshpots of Berlin
in your day. Fraulein Schröder's guesthouse.

A naughty, gossipy, big-hearted place bursting at the seams
with rumours of the hour and news bulletins from the streets.
No 17, Nollendorfstrasse. A pale yellow house

with pigeons sitting on the sunny balconies today,
a calm peaceful Sunday, the city in bloom.
Standing at your door, hot tears begin to flow

as you take shape in my mind's eye, revealing yourself
within me though I only know you from the pages of books
when first we met in *Goodbye to Berlin* some thirty years ago.

I see you in that room, the patina of heavy Prussian furniture
around you as you keenly bring to artistic life
that easygoing bohemian family

with whom you shared your lodgings in the early Thirties;
sympathetic characters chiselled for all time—
Mr Norris, Fraulein Schröder, the lovely foolish Sally Bowles.

I'm at your doorstep but other tenants live here now,
Weiss and Wagner, Miller and Bretner,
but it's not them that I see but you; the sharp look

as you take me in; nothing escapes you;
the same acuity that illumined Berlin in the early years
of its tumult. Impressionable Berlin of indolence. Poor famine-stricken Berlin.

'I'm a camera,' you said yourself and never spoke a truer word
capturing as you did every live moment of the city
in the fluency of your word-lens as the hour of dread

drew nigh; Nazis and their brutish entourage making a name
for themselves; bullying and badgering on the streets;
aggressive demonstrations, defiant assemblies, whipping up of frenzy,

the swagger of it all and Hitler, cock o' the dungheap, crowing all the way to
the Reichstag. You caught it, Christopher,
the city you loved and all her charms going down the drain.

Here I am at your doorstep and though you are but dust of the earth
there's a spring in your step as you rush down the stairs to greet me
 bright eyes brimful of roguery.

And off we go through the streets of Berlin: Eisenacher.
Motzstrasse, Fuggerstrasse, and their numerous bars
with gorgeous blue-eyed untameable boys, Christopher,

the type you always liked, sweet heart,
Otto, Bubi, Heinz; here they come with a welcoming grin.
In this age of licence, no shy wallflowers these

strutting their stuff with the best of them, tattling peacocks
in Blue Boy, Tom's House, Pussycat and Pinnochio.
'Life is a cabaret, old chum', you say before you vanish from my dream.

I salute you, Christopher. How you embraced the world
In those champagne days and nights before Hitler crucified
the gay cabarets, the rumpy-rumpy with fellow-angels.

And when the tyranny was too much to bear
you said goodbye to Berlin, yourself and the heart-melting, gentle Heinz
searching for asylum here, there and everywhere

across Europe and finding no luck;
and when he was arrested in the end, your heart was in smithereens.
And I understand your loss for I, too, know what it is,

what is broken and torn when lovers part;
but you kept going and the light of humanity radiated from your words
flowing gracefully through the vein of narratives.

Here I am at your door, Christopher, the blessed door of solace
for me and others who come here to worship you.
You who beatified
our queer lives, here's a word-posy for you, respectfully yours.

The Pub on a Saturday Night, Cricklewood, 1972

They came: the one on his own,
the lonely one and the one who didn't belong anywhere,
wild men, bruised men
men of good cheer, men fit to be tied
 the digger of ditches and thieving ganger,
dirty old men and innocent young fellows.

They came from mean inhospitable lodgings
and desolate joyless rooms
they came in their Sunday best and in tatters,
they came newly combed and washed, they came in filth
handsome they came and ugly,
they came for some peace in the refuge of the alehouse.

They came with the melancholy of being caught between two countries,
They came with the torment of cities
to get stark raving drunk they came, to numb their sadness
they came with treachery brewing in the mind, looking for revenge
they came to defend their good name and to strike a blow
they came to lose their desolation in the throng
they came to lodge their tribulations in self-pity.

They came to flee life.

Servant Girl

Walking outside in the morning
a gentle summer mist
as soft and smooth
as a rabbit's fur
or the fresh fragrant
graceful linen
that I carefully lay
on the priest's pleasing bed.

Mandelstam on his Deathbed

I challenged the mob
that dismissed poetry
as a feckless hobby

I spoke of things
forbidden to be told
in this time of infamy

Stalin, czar of horror,
drew my blood
for exposing his twisted ways

But from my death wounds
words will flow in a spate of truth
to damn him for all eternity.

I challenged the tyrant
that suppressed my writings.
My songs will be sung when he lies dumb in the earth.

from *An Bhé Ghlas*, 2015

Sunday in Mín 'a Leá, Sunday in Gaza

A gentle Sunday
in Mín 'a Leá
I'm unperturbed
in the garden
my counterpart in Gaza
running out of breath
pleading
to escape
the next missile attack
the fallout of explosions.

A soft slow sleepy Sunday
in Mín 'a Leá
night will fall into silence
a moon will rise
relaxing in the air
but in Gaza
the sky will ignite
in burning flames
houses will crumble
bones shatter.

On this quiet Sunday
in Mín 'a Leá
how easy it is
to mourn Gaza
as I sit in the garden
comfortably
enjoying the scent
of newly cut grass
not a care in the world
but the making of a poem.

Not a care in the world
but the making of a poem?

To Mohammed Abu Khdeir

A Palestinian boy burnt alive in the woods outside Jerusalem

Your little shapely-carved faced
bony as a bird's;
a green linnet or dove.

Light-footed as a gust of breeze
and lithe, supple
as a sally rod.

That morning, like other days,
you delighted your father and mother
with your blossoming smile

Before setting off for the mosque
to perform your rituals,
the kneeling and bowing required by the Book.

But, dear one, they whisked you away
to the woods; bloodthirsty delinquents
reared on the testament of revenge

To pay for the youths of their own race
treacherously murdered, they sought what was theirs.
You were condemned, dear heart, on the altar of blood.

I see you with your youthful locks flowing,
flames engulfing your limbs,
your sixteen years of loveliness in torment.

Your innards explode
like acorns, sinews
ripped apart as they burn you alive.

The Sacred Books are wilting,
bent low in shame,
the words of the prophets splattered and stained with your
blood.

Today the world is blanched, morning
is a grey dove, I hear the savage moan
of your blood, in Palestine of many a weary heart.

Mohammed Abu Khdeir, every letter
of your name, sweet innocent child,
cries out forever in the congealed alphabet of pain.

The Berry Hollow of Lag na Sméar

Here are blackberries
  in seductive clusters
  in heavy tresses

Numberless berries
  soaked in the earth's blood
  and fired by the sun

Neat produce of tangled briars;
  soft juice of autumnal days
  wayside banquet

There they hang, full of lure
  blushing purple—
  a generous spread

My passions are aroused
  and prick me as they like
  I must have them!

Wild and bloodthirsty
  a matter of life and death
  each juicy mouthful

I cannot overcome their charms!
  every year I plunge my fangs
  into their pulsing veins

Their sweet soft bloodiness.
  To pass them by
  without tasting them

Would send me into paroxysms
   of starvation.
      Delicious, swollen, lascivious

I fondle them
   in the palm of my hand.
      Demon of Gluttony am I

The vampire
   that licks their pulchritude
      with blood-smeared tongue

And how miserable I am
   when their sheen is gone
      when old age disfigures them

As November drags on
   the fairy people do their business
      and the bushes stink to the high heavens

Essay

Fuadach eachtardhomhandach i nDún na nGall

Níl a fhios agam cén Ghaeilge atá ar *alien abduction*. Fuadach eachtardhomhandach, ab ea? N'fheadar an dtarlaíonn a leithéid in aon chor nó an samhlaíocht ar fad é? Go maithe Dia dhom é ach nár bhreá leat dá bhfuadódh na heachtardhomhandaigh cuid de dhomhandaigh Dháil Éireann agus an tSeanaid. B'fhéidir go bhfoghlaimeodh an dream seo againne cleas nó dhó ó na spásairí chun sinn a tharraingt as an abar ina bhfuilimid.

Déarfadh síciatraithe gur dócha gur scitsifréine nó hipearmáine nó galar intinne éigin a bhí ar mháthair Chathail Uí Shearcaigh, bean a chaith a lán ama i measc na sióg, mas fíor di féin. Rith sé liomsa gur fuadach eachtardhomhandach a tharla di. An cuntas a fhaighimid ar mháthair an fhile an chuid is corraithí dá chuimhní cinn, *Light on Distant Hills*, a d'fhoilsigh Simon & Schuster sa bhliain 2009. Is trua nach i nGaeilge a scríobhadh é. Níl an Béarla rómhaith ag déileáil leis an saol eile.

Deir an t-údar, 'My mother was an inveterate traveller in the other-world; a regular visitor to unearthly parts.' Tá go leor sa mhéid sin. Nílimid lánchinnte an taistealaí in aghaidh a tola ab ea í nó nach ea. An léir dúinn ón abairt thuas cad é an saol eile seo go díreach agus conas dul isteach is amach ann? Cuairteoir rialta ab ea í. Cuairteoir. Faoi mar ba rud nádúrtha é. Bothántaíocht. Airneán. Agus cad is brí le 'unearthly'? Neamhshaolta? Eachtardhomhandach?

Dhein an Searcach an-iarracht go deo chun tuiscint a fháil ar ghalar a mháthar. Ach cá bhfios nach galar ach bua é a bheith in ann cuairt a thabhairt ar chríochaibh neamhshaolta. Agus ar aon chuma, nach bhfuil litríocht agus béaloideas na tíre seo ag cur thar maoil le tagairtí don saol eile? Tá ar ndóigh.

Anois, má dhein eachtardhomhandaigh tú a fhuadach, ná téir i dteagmháil liomsa mar gheall air. Le do thoil. Ná scríobh chugam.

Ná cuir glao teileafóin orm. (Níl fón póca agam, mar a tharlaíonn, agus is annamh a fhreagraím an fón sa halla. An uair dheireanach a d'fhreagraíos an fón bhí fónaí éigin ag iarraidh fón nua a dhíol liom). Ná cuir ríomhphost chugam. Ní bheidh mé in ann comhairle do leasa a chur ort. Is dóigh le daoine áirithe má scríobhann tú aiste nó dhó don Irish Times go gcaithfidh go bhfuil meáchan céille agat. Is éadrom-mheáchan mé fad is a bhaineann sé le fuadach eachtardhomhandach, bíodh an méid sin soiléir.

Bíonn daoine ag scríobh chugam, an dtuigeann tú. Is dóigh liom gur eachtardhomhandaigh is ea cuid acu. An bhféadfainn labhairt amach faoi seo nó siúd, an bhféadfainn alt a scríobh mar gheall ar XYZ—scannal!—caithfidh duine éigin scríobh mar gheall air. Bhuel, a deirimse, labhair amach ina thaobh tú féin. Nó fostaigh púca pinn. Ní hin an Ghaeilge oifigiúil ar 'ghost writer' ach scáthscríbhneoir. Ach cad tá cearr le púca pinn? Nach ceart go mbeadh vóta againn? Cén fáth a bhfuil an focal 'scáthscríbhneoir' againn? Téarmaíocht éigeantach! Tá vóta uainn! Tá guth uainn! Saoirse!

Bhí ainmneacha ag máthair an tSearcaigh ar an slua sí. Ní haon dream amháin iad na daoine maithe (más maith atá siad). Tá scata acu ann, mar a bheadh treibheanna ann. Slua díobh b'as Caor an Airgid iad. Rud nach bhfuil soiléir in aon chor ón leabhar ná an méid seo: an raibh an t-ainm sin, agus ainmneacha eile nach iad, i mbéal na ndaoine nó an i mbéal mháthair Chathail amháin a bhí siad? Más i mbéal a mháthar amháin a bhíodar, cá bhfuair sise iad mar ainmneacha? Ar chum sí an t-ainm Caor an Airgid? Gar do Shliabh Sneachta atá Caor an Airgid ach níl sé ar aon mhapa. Ar mhapa aigne mháthair an fhile a bhí sé agus is soiléir a bhí sé ann.

Tá leabhar filíochta ag an Athair Micheál de Liostún dar teideal *Screadfaidh na Clocha Amach*. Thuig máthair Chathail caint na gcloch. Dúirt sí leis uair amháin go raibh cloch tar éis a rá léi go raibh gála chucu ó Ghleann Tornáin. Agus b'fhíor don chloch. Ba ghearr go raibh sé ina ghála. Cuimhnigh ar éifeacht na tairngreachta sin ar gharsún óg.

Bhí sáreolas ag máthair Chathail ar an Eall, abhainn, ar Agall, áit chnocánach, Donn an Domhain, áit sceirdiúil neamhthorthúil, Pulc, cathair an óir, Ball na mBuacán, cathair thoirmiscthe. Istoíche a raghfá go dtí na háiteanna sin. Ní fhéadfá dul ann faoi sholas an lae. Na háiteanna sin go léir, tíreolas agus logainmneacha na n-áiteanna dofheicthe sin, tá draíocht mhillteanach ag baint leo: Tulc, Ruacan, Fán, Daol, Ston, Idir Eatarthu (an ceann is deise liom), Dearg na gCorr agus Scan.

Bhíodh an slua sí ag glaoch uirthi. Dúirt sí lena maicín óg uair amháin go raibh báibín as Co. na Gaillimhe fuadaithe ag lucht Chaor an Airgid agus go rabhadar ag glaoch uirthi mar go raibh banaltra chíche uathu. Nuair a cheistíodh Cathal í faoi na háiteanna sin is é a deireadh sí ná gur ar imeall neamhní a bhíodar.

Bhí cónaí ar neacha fadghéagacha i nDearg na gCorr, tuairim is seacht n-oíche siar uathu. Ní i slata ná i mílte a deineadh an t-aistear a thomhas ach ina oícheanta. Bhíodh saghas ióga ar siúl ag na neacha sin chun an domhan glioscarnach ina mhaireadar a chaomhnú agus a íonghlanadh. Ba nós leo seasamh ar chos amháin ar feadh trí lá in abhainn gheal, leathshúil leo druidte agus iad ag cantaireacht. Bhí púdar draíochta acu a dheineadar as beacáin agus caora dearga, púdar a d'iompraítí i bpúitse agus a dtugtar 'bolg an tsolais' agus bhí gá acu le duine daonna chun an bunábhar a bhailiú. Agnes, mathair Chathail, an duine sin. Bhí uirthi na muisiriúin agus na caora a mheilt ansin le tuairgnín airgid. Mheascadh saoi ansin ina phúdar é thuas in Inis Ór na gCorr, oileán spéire. Is bhí na neacha sin ar a sáimhín suilt agus caor na mbeacán, mar a thug Agnes ar an gcógas, á ghlacadh acu gach lá.

Dhein na neacha osnádúrtha sin Agnes a ghlanadh sula ligfí isteach i ríocht an tsolais í. Bhíodh sí cuachta faoi scragall geal de shaghhas éigin agus chuirtí isteach i ngléas gaile ansin í lena sciomradh agus nuair a thagadh sí amach bhíodh sí chomh geal le scilling nua. Ní go dtí sin a a ligtí di dul ag piocadh na gcaor is na mbeacán.

Agus conas a bhain sí na háiteanna sin amach? Fuair sí síob, a duirt sí, ó dhath. An dath gorm. Is fearr ná ficsean a bheadh bunaithe ar fhuadach eachtardhomhandach an cuntas éachtach a thugann Cathal dúinn ar aistir dhiamhra a mháthar. Ach an ficsean é? Nó an bhfuil fírinne ann, fírinne atá ceilte ar dhaoine normálta? Léigh an leabhar. Nílimse chun a thuilleadh a rá.

Gabriel Rosenstock

www.ingramcontent.com/pod-product-compliance
Lightning Source LLC
LaVergne TN
LVHW091153080426
835509LV00006B/659